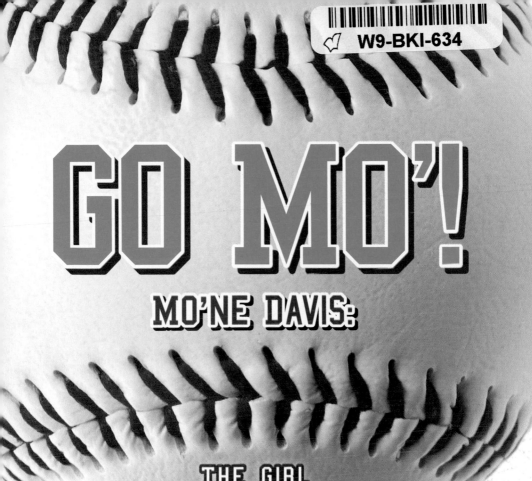

GO MO'!

MO'NE DAVIS:

THE GIRL
WHO CHANGED
BASEBALL HISTORY

BY
JOE BUBAR

SCHOLASTIC INC

UNAUTHORIZED:
This book is not sponsored by or affiliated with
Mo'ne Davis or anyone associated with her.

© 2015 by Scholastic
ISBN 978-0-545-83753-8

Published by Scholastic Inc.
SCHOLASTIC and associated logos are trademarks
and/or registered trademarks of Scholastic Inc.

12 11 10   17 18 19 20/0

Printed in the U.S.A.   40
First printing, January 2015

Table of CONTENTS

MEET MO'NE

The crowd was on its feet. The stadium was rocking. People were chanting, "Mo-nay, Mo-nay, Mo-nay!" It was the first round of the 2014 Little League World Series, the nationally televised tournament for the world's top youth baseball players. And on August 15, 2014, a 13-year-old girl named Mo'ne Davis was about to make history.

Mo'ne was one strike away from becoming the first girl ever to pitch her team to victory in the Little League World Series. Even better, she was throwing a shutout—meaning she had yet to allow the other team to score.

Mo'ne's team, the Taney Dragons of Philadelphia, Pennsylvania, were winning the game 4–0. Mo'ne had already struck out the first two batters of the sixth and final inning. Now, she stared down the third hitter. She wound up, kicked her leg high, and fired the pitch. The ball whizzed by the batter. The umpire yelled, "Strike three!"

Mo'ne had done it! She had just made history.

That game not only made the record books. It also made Mo'ne one of the biggest sports stars of 2014. But her journey was unexpected—and it was just beginning.

NO GIRLS ALLOWED

Mo'ne never would have been able to play in the Little League World Series if not for another girl named Maria Pepe. In 1972, Maria pitched in three Little League games in Hoboken, New Jersey. But then she was asked to leave the team. At that time, girls weren't allowed to play Little League baseball.

Maria refused to back down, though. The National Organization for Women took her case to the New Jersey State Supreme Court. In 1974, the court ruled that Little League must let girls play ball alongside boys.

Maria paved the way for girls, like Mo'ne, to play Little League baseball. But even today, girls are greatly outnumbered by boys in Little League. In the 67-year-history of the Little League World Series, only 18 players have been girls. And none of them made history quite like Mo'ne.

Maria Pepe, female Little League baseball pioneer.

MO'NE IS DISCOVERED

Mo'ne's story begins when she was seven years old. One day, she was throwing a football with her cousins and older brother. A man named Steve Bandura was nearby. He saw her throw one perfect spiral after another to darting receivers. He also watched her chase down the much older and larger boys, and tackle them.

Steve worked at a recreation center in Philadelphia. He had seen a lot of young athletes. But watching Mo'ne that day, he knew that she was special.

Steve went up to Mo'ne and invited her to come watch a boys' basketball practice at the rec center. But when Mo'ne showed up to the practice, she didn't just watch. She jumped right in. She ran through basketball drills perfectly—even though it was the first time she had ever done them. It was clear that Mo'ne was a natural athlete!

PRACTICE MAKES PERFECT

Mo'ne soon started playing baseball, too. She worked with Coach Steve on her pitching. She practiced her leg kick and her balance. She trained herself to keep her eyes on the target. In the summer of 2014, all of her hard work paid off. She made the Taney Dragons select team and they won the Pennsylvania State championship.

The Dragons then traveled to Bristol, Connecticut, to compete in the Mid-Atlantic Regional Tournament. The winner of the tournament would go to the Little League World Series. But winning regionals wasn't going to be easy. The Dragons were up against other state champions from all over the East Coast.

MO'NE IN THE REGIONALS

Mo'ne was up to the challenge. In her first game pitching in the regionals, she struck out ten batters!

Mo'ne next pitched in the championship game of the Mid-Atlantic Regional Tournament. For six innings, she fired 70-mile-per-hour fastballs by hitters. She made the batters' knees buckle with each curveball she threw. Mo'ne only allowed three hits. The other team didn't score a run.

The Taney Dragons won the game 8–0. They were crowned the champions of the Mid-Atlantic region.

Next, the Dragons traveled to Williamsport, Pennsylvania. That's the home of the Little League World Series. It's also where Mo'ne was about to make national headlines.

MO'NE MAKES HISTORY

On August 15, Mo'ne took the mound and tried to pretend like it was any other game. But this wasn't just any game. After all, it was the Little League World Series. There were television crews all over, a ballpark announcer, and music blaring from a loudspeaker. The stands were packed with a roaring crowd. It looked and felt a lot like a Major League Baseball game.

But Mo'ne is one cool kid. She never let the pressure get to her. She blocked out the crowd and took deep breaths before each pitch. She told herself, "Just throw strikes."

That's exactly what she did. She struck out six batters and held the other team scoreless. When the game ended, and the Taney Dragons won 4–0, Mo'ne's name went down in the record books.

MO'NE IS A STAR

After that game, Mo'ne became one of the summer's biggest sports stars. Huge crowds followed her wherever she went. Mo'ne signed autographs for kids and even adults.

Mo'ne wasn't just a pitcher. She also played first base and hit for the Dragons. In the team's second game of the Little League World Series, she hit a run-scoring single. She became only the sixth girl ever to get a hit in the Little League World Series.

Mo'ne was best known for her pitching, though. She pitched again in the team's third game of the Little League World Series. A crowd of more than 34,000 people showed up to watch her take the mound. That's a bigger crowd than you'd see at a lot of Major League Baseball games! Many spectators had to stand because there weren't enough seats in the

stadium. Some fans wore T-shirts that said
"Go, Mo!"

Millions more people were watching the game
on television. In fact, the game broke the
record for the most TV viewers for a Little
League World Series game.

The Dragons lost the game, and were
eliminated from the tournament the next day.
But Mo'ne had done something even greater
than winning a baseball game. She had become
an inspiration to girls all over the country
who dream of playing ball in the Little
League World Series!

THE LIFE OF A CELEBRITY

On August 25, 2014 , Mo'ne's own dream came true. She was looking at one of her favorite magazines, *Sports Illustrated*. On the front cover, she expected to see a photograph of a professional athlete. But instead, her picture was on the cover! Mo'ne had just made history again—as the youngest person ever on the magazine's cover.

Having her photograph on the cover of *Sports Illustrated* was just one of many magical moments for Mo'ne during the summer of 2014. She was all over ESPN, she appeared on talk shows, and she met celebrities. She also marched with her team through the streets of Philadelphia in a parade that was held in their honor.

REMEMBER HER NAME

Mo'ne had one busy summer. She broke down barriers for girls, set records in the Little League World Series, and became an instant celebrity.

But her story isn't over. She plans to keep playing baseball. The next time you read about her, though, it might be for a different sport. Believe it or not, Mo'ne says basketball is her best sport. Her goal is to one day play college basketball at the University of Connecticut.

MO'NE
Summer Scrapbook

Mo'ne on parad[e]
to celebrate th[e]
championship,
August 27, 20[1]

Mo'ne throws
the first pitch
at a Los Angeles
Dodgers game

Kevin Frandsen
of the Washingt[on]
Nationals

Mo'ne meets WNBA All-Star Maya
Moore before a playoff game

Mo'ne and her team meet the Philadelphia Phillies before a game

Mo'ne is
interviewed
by reporters

#MO'NE ON TWITTER

Mo'ne made a lot of fans during the Little League World Series. Many famous people praised her on Twitter:

NBA Most Valuable Player Kevin Durant

Kevin Durant ✓
@KDTrey5

〔 Follow 〕

This youngster is striking everybody out and she is a girl. I love it. #itsanewday

4:53 PM - 15 Aug 2014

The First Lady ✓
@FLOTUS

〔 Follow 〕

Congrats to Mo'ne Davis on becoming the first girl to pitch an #LLWS shutout. When girls succeed, we all succeed. #yhoo.it/1uZ3cdA

12:30 PM - 16 Aug 2014

First Lady Michelle Obama

Baseball All-Star Mike Trout

Mike Trout ✓
@Trouty20

〔 Follow 〕

Mo'ne Davis is straight dominating...fun to watch !!! #LLWS #MidAtlantic

4:30 PM - 15 Aug 2014

David Price ✓
@DAVIDprice14

Follow

Baseball
All-Star
David Price

Mo'ne Davis is a stud!!! I'll be watching whenever she pitches for sure!! 3 hit shutout to go to the World Series!!! #baller

1:59 PM - 11 Aug 2014

Senator Pat Toomey ✓
@SenToomey

Follow

#MoneDavis was terrific tonight for the #TaneyDragons. Perfect 4-6-3 DP to win it. Now on to Williamsport at the @ LittleLeague World Series!

US Senator
for Pennsylvania
Pat Toomey

7:58 PM - 10 Aug 2014

andrew mccutchen ✓
@TheCUTCH22

Follow

MLB Most
Valuable Player
Andrew
McCutchen

S/O to PA, and @MoneDavis11. Rooting for you guys over here!#LLWS2014

4:11 PM - 15 Aug 2014

Earvin Magic Johnson ✓
@MagicJohnson

Follow

Who said girls can't play baseball? Yesterday, Mo'ne Davis threw complete game shut out to lead her team to the #LLWS!

Basketball Hall
of Famer Magic
Johnson

5:31 PM - 11 Aug 2014

Russell Wilson ✓
@DangeRussWilson

Follow

Super Bowl
Champion
Russell Wilson

This is so cool! Congrats Mo'ne Davis on the outstanding pitching performance. Keep it up! #WhyNotYou

11:44 AM - 11 Aug 2014

MO'NE'S STATS AT THE LITTLE LEAGUE WORLD SERIES

TANEY **DRAGONS**

MO'NE DAVIS

PITCHER

MO'NE DAVIS

PITCHER

CHARACTER · COURAGE · LOYALTY

LITTLE LEAGUE BASEBALL

IP 8.1	W 1	H 8	ER 3	K 14
GS 2	L 1	R 3	BB 1	ERA 2.16

KEY

IP: Innings pitched
GS: Games started as a pitcher
W: Wins
L: Losses
H: Hits allowed
R: Runs allowed
ER: Earned runs allowed
BB: Base on balls (walks) allowed
K: Strikeouts
ERA: Earned Run Average

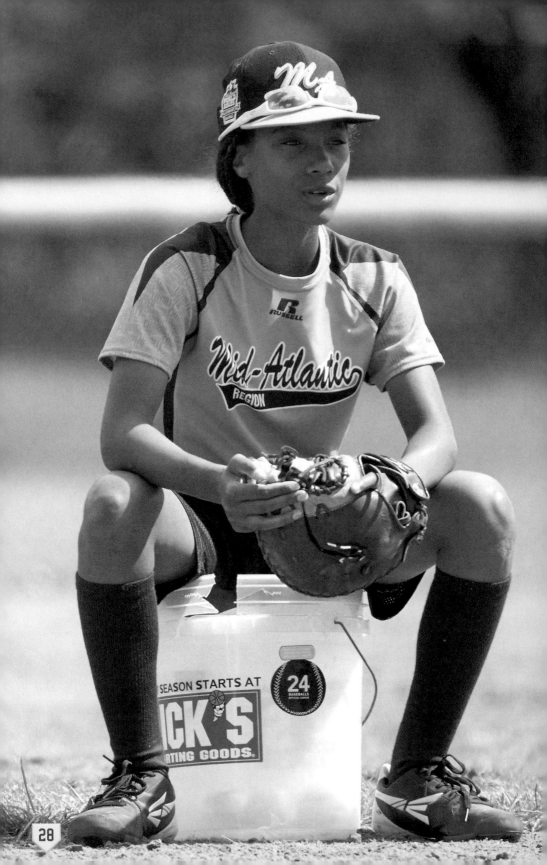

MO'NE FACT SHEET

Nickname: Mo

Height: 5' 4"

Throws: Right-handed

Bats: Right-handed

Pitches: Fastball, curveball, changeup, knuckleball

Fastball Top Speed: 70 miles per hour

Lucky Charm: Keeps money in her back pocket

Favorite Baseball Player: Chase Utley

Favorite Athlete: LeBron James

Favorite Food: Pizza

Favorite Movie: Cheaper by the Dozen

Celebrity She'd Most Like To Meet: Selena Gomez

Favorite Walk Up Song: "Run the World (Girls)" by Beyoncé

The Ultimate Q&A WITH MO'NE

What do you think of all the attention you've gotten?

Sometimes it can be fun. Sometimes I really don't like it. It's a lot for a 13-year-old girl, and I don't think people know that. So they keep coming, asking questions. They don't know how it's a lot for one person.

Describe to me the feeling the moment you first saw yourself on the cover of *Sports Illustrated*.

I was very shocked. But I was excited at the same time because I always wanted to be on that. To be on it right now is really cool.

How do you handle all the pressure and stay focused when you're on the mound?

I just take deep breaths and I tell myself to just throw strikes.

What was your favorite part about being in the Little League World Series?

My favorite part was playing on the fields. The grounds crew made them really nice, and just looking at the fields was so cool.

What did it feel like to have more than 30,000 people in the stands watching you?

I didn't really pay attention to a lot if I was pitching or playing because that would throw me off. But it was cool to see how many people were there to cheer on our team.

How have your teammates helped you feel at home on the team?

We laugh a lot and we make jokes a lot and just laugh a lot during the games.

Do you view yourself as a role model for other girls?

Yes, just by doing positive things. When you do positive things, it influences others to do positive things.

Would you like to see more girls in Little League?

Yes. A lot of people came up to me and said that their daughter wanted to play baseball. And I told them they should let her play.

What advice would you give to other girls who want to play baseball?

Just go out there and play.

What do you think is a mistake a lot of young pitchers make?

That they have to strike out every batter. Just throw strikes. When you try to strike out every batter, you kind of overpower it and you won't throw a lot of strikes. So just stay calm and throw strikes.

How did you learn how to pitch?

I learned from Coach Steve. He taught me a lot about mechanics. The key is to keep your eye on the target.

Have you ever had to adjust your pitching mechanics or style? How?
    I kept working on my mechanics. I worked on my balance a lot. When
    I did the leg lift, I would just keep my leg up to see how long I could
    stay up.

Who is your favorite teacher—non-coach? And why? How did he/she
help you learn?
    Ms. Joy because she's fun. We have fun in her class. It's art class,
    and she taught us how to make cartoons and how to make certain
    things. It's really fun.

Is there a book that influenced you to read? Why?
    Probably Divergent. I saw the movie and the movie was really good
    so I wanted to see the difference between them.